A Map of Flames

A Map of Flames

Poems

PAMMY SACHER KOHLI

TIGER PRINT

An imprint of Speaking Tiger Publishing

SPEAKING TIGER PUBLISHING PVT. LTD
4381/4, Ansari Road, Daryaganj
New Delhi 110002

First published in India in Tigerprint by Speaking Tiger 2018

ISBN: 978-93-88326-10-0

10 9 8 7 6 5 4 3 2 1

Typeset in Garamond Premier Pro by SÜRYA, New Delhi
Printed at Sanat Printers, Kundli

'Be thine own palace, or the world's thy jail.'
—John Donne

'Home Over the Rainbow'. Georgetown (Washington, D.C.), April 2001.

Contents

Silver Arrow

No longing
No desire
A feeling of love
In a festoon
Of bougainvillea flowers
Hanging by my window.

The early sun's rays
Wrap the dawn
In a golden shawl
And my beloved's voice
Comes to me in the koel's call.

I emerge into sunrise
Kisses, a smile
Riding a silver arrow
From the golden heart
Of my beloved to mine.

Rain

To awaken to rain
Through closed doors
And run to open the window
With half shut eyes

And breathe the scent
Of wet earth
Green leaves washed clean
On trees, shrubs
In the perfect temperatures
Of a bit of heaven in Delhi
The whore the bride the prize
Every conqueror has eyed

Renewed again by monsoon rain.

Wet

Sparkling waves
Gently swelling exhaling
Rippling ashore
Rising falling
Lulling a longing in the soul

Soothing senses
Unquenched bruised and worn.

Wilful water
Unfurling running laughing
Leaping chasing
Like children at play
Then melting

With a soft hiss
Gently kissing encircling
Our feet pushing sand
Between our toes
Slipping tickling
Shifting retreating
Silently back to the ocean
To the ocean floor
Leaving a smooth urgent
Rhythm in our bodies.

Sand upon our legs
Sand in our hair
And clouds shedding rivers

Monsoon rain falling
Upon our shoulders and heads
A wet happy union
Carved in hard black rock

In an ancient cave
The imprint of your face
Your shape traced
Beneath my fingers
Every bulge hollow crevice
Forever engraved
Upon my brain.

The Ganga Train

I hear the rocking
Rhythm of the train
The sound of grinding
Rolling metal wheels
And a dull deep whistle
Blowing in the night.

Setting out on a far journey
High above the Ganga
Wondering what there was
If anything in it for me.
Knowing only it was thrilling
To be with you
On a midnight train I'd dreamed of
All my life.

I hear the huffing puffing
Gasping train pulling out
Of steamy station lights
Leaving urchin calls
Of 'Chaa-aa-ai chai
Garam chai' behind
And piercing the darkness
Chasing the moon into daylight
Sliding past village wells

Sun-baked huts
Of mud and cracked clay
And walls spotted with pats
Of cow dung and chopped hay.

Whistling on
Slipping silently along
Open fields of scrub and thorn
And slender reeds fast asleep
In moonlit ponds
Shadows of gigantic ghosts
Dancing among groves of trees
Leaping and fleeing
Into the distant hills.

Moonbeams pouring in through
Our carriage window
Transforming the whites of our sheets
Shirts and pillows
With a luminescent glow.
We lie calm and still
Nestled close in the hush of night
Listening on twin headphones
To haunting echoes of Ravel's Bolero.
Bridging gaps and breathing peace
In our hearts and minds.
You reach out gently

For my hand
And enclose it firmly
In yours.

I hear the rocking
Rhythm of the train
The sound of grinding
Rolling metal wheels
And a dull deep whistle
Blowing in the night.

Calling

I hear you calling out to me
Like a creature in the night
Your silent words disclose your fancy
A meaning known to you only.

I know you believe in me
Your love flows in me
Like a mountain stream
A force against resistance.
Your caring wraps my entirety
And fills dry empty spaces
Of hurt and agony.

I hear you calling in the night
I wait I listen to the eternity
Of a breath of hope
Unfolding somewhere inside me.

Dawn

Shimmering
On silvery ocean waves
Kissing golden sand

Glistening
On virgin sheets
Of snow-clad mountains
Slipping
Onto rocky slopes
Orange red yellow
On Green violet blue.

Painting
Glowing black silhouettes
Of camel riders
On pearl-white dunes
Endless waves of sand.

Dawn.

Another Dawn

White rolling clouds
In blue mountain ranges—
O naked valley of sunshine gold
Body clad and transparent soul
This must be where it began:
Wild flowers from the garden
Picked by her prince
For her with love.

So lilting laughter flows over
Tennis lawns and polo grounds
Cognac and billiard rounds
Ancient antlers on club walls
And a sign on the bar that says
'Children not allowed.'

O princess, princess
All grown up
And come so far
To go where you please
Do as you wish
And lost in love
With your prince of charm.

Cigar fumes and bridge tables
Dancing couples swaying in the hall
Blazing fires of pine wood and cones
Casting shadows on regal rugs
And up to the walls.

A double staircase
Leading to a piano room
A parlour for tea
A dining and powder room
A bedroom measuring
Forty feet by sixty
And a bath with a tub so big
It takes three servants to fill
For her prince to soak in.

High above a royal bed
Gigantic arches span
Age-old rafters spread
In a symmetrical plan
Glowing in candlelight
Kindling dreams
Deep into the night
Filled with trust and warm delight
Taking wing and flying
Into the ruby rust
And aquamarine
Of a Himalayan dawn.

Indian Sky

In the silence where I lie
Falling asleep in the night
Beneath a blushing Indian sky
Fragrant breezes
Of champa, chameli
Madhumalti and shiuli
Pass gently by.
And you whisper to me
Everything will be all right.

Thank you for your loving
Advice on the smallest of things
On walking standing sitting
And sleeping properly
How what when and where
To eat and drink
How to dress what to wear
And sometimes even how to think.

I want to tell you it is fun
To be with you
Through thick and thin
The best and worst of people
Places times and things.

You take away the pain
And bring back my smile again
You're the sunshine and the rain
You keep me calm through the storm
You're the reason for living on
To greet a new day at sunrise.

Singing in the Wilderness

I see a million flowers
Blooming in the wilderness
Where we walked
Laughed and talked
Through golden hours.
You picked the prettiest flowers
And carefully blending their colours
Gave them to me lovingly.

Waking up early one morning
I kissed you softly
As you lay sleeping
Thanking heavens for keeping
You safely with me.
I kept remembering the black
Hot waters bubbling deep
Within the dark cold currents
Of the Jumna River
Flowing swiftly in its steep
Sharp valley through mountains
Of such isolation
That I held you back
from swimming
In its frothing swirling
Tempting waters.

It was much too horrifying
To think of separating
From you even momentarily
Let alone losing you forever
In the desolation
Of that primeval river.

Grateful and glad to touch
And feel you beside me
I left you sleeping
And went skipping
In the early hours
To my enchanting valley
Of wild flowers.

The mountain air
Kissed my face and hair
And the sun
As it was dawning
Sparked the crimson
White and golden shades
Of countless flowers
Spreading their fragrance
And blossoming just for you
That October morning.

My heart expanded with love
Overflowing in above around me
And bursting everywhere.
I gathered armfuls of flowers
In their glory
And carried them to you
With all my care.

Their fragrance fills me still
As I close my eyes
And once again feel
The mountain air
Kiss my face and hair
And you beside me
Singing in the wilderness.

Starry Skies

Take me for a moment
Before the embers
That leap out to you
Die in their ashes.

Kindle the flame
To burst and burn
To blazing passion
Stirring a dying spirit
To move dance and sing
Bare beneath the sun
Moon and stars
To the rhythm of millions of rocks
Rolling in riverbeds.

Submit to love
Eternal ephemeral like stars
Exploding imploding
More ancient than God
You and me burning
In the sky.

Back to School

All summer long we spent
Days with the flowers
Catching butterflies
Chasing dragonflies over
Smooth pebbles along
Streams riverbanks and ponds.

Playing make-believe
My sister said
I'm Lily and you are Rose
Marigolds are Guruji's flowers
So my favorite colour is yellow
And yours is red.

Squeezing my cheeks
Between finger and thumb
She said
Don't be sad
My little gogi
My yummy yolk of egg
I'll soon return and bring for you
A toffee a lollypop a sugar stick—
And back to school she went.

Car to Kasauli, 1947

Did she dare disturb the motherland?
To return at the close
To look for roots to rest her head
In a land she calls her own?

Bulldozers came along
To destroy her home again
Wasn't once enough to be driven
Out of her ancestral land
Clutching her doll to her chest
Hanging on to her sister's hand
And traversing a refugee camp
In her city's cantonment?

Sounds of wailing in her ears
Her baby eyes seeing unseeing
Unfamiliar billows rising
Curling black thick
And turning thin grey cold
Sniffing the sick
Stench of smouldering brick
And cinders screaming
Rape! Loot! Hack! Slash!

Blood! Death! Come too soon
Too fast. All at once
Just like that.

Little girls and older
Women young and old
Weeping wailing with their tresses
Crudely shorn off by sword
Cut and chopped by scissors
Or torn out by hand.

Babies born unborn with none
To hold them or for them
To hold on to and travel far
Far from that maddened lot.

She saw heard and forgot
For she was not old enough
To know it was lucky to have got
Pulled along carried perhaps asleep
In the car from her home
Beside a church in Rawalpindi
To a houseful of roses
Beside a church in Kasauli.

Away from her land of five fertile rivers

Sutlej Ravi Beas Jhelum Chenab
Fed by dove-white Himalayan snows
That flow due west even to this day
She's told.

Shivo Hum

The dance of Shiva
Bhum bhum
The chant of Shiva
Bhum bhum.

East West North South
Tigers jungles bhang
In all diversity of colour
And entirety
I am One
Bhum bhum.

I am Om
Namo Shiva
Shiva Namo Om
Bhum bhum.

Bholenath
Jai Shiva Omkara
Shivo hum Shivo hum
Bhum bhum.

Tropics

Born in the tropics I awaken to the sun
At four, five fifteen, six fifteen or seven
I know it's rising from the glow
In my window
It lights up my third eye
With the vibrant tilak of life
In a kaleidoscope's burst of colour.

Kulfi

Out on a lark
Among the milling crowds
Of a summer's eve
By the side street
In Pandara Park
Sizzling tikkas seekh kababs
Rumali roti tandoori naan.

In the mood
For matke-waali kulfi
With sweet slippery falooda.
Banarasi paan
On rose petals in a silver thaali
On a mid-summer's eve
In New Delhi.

Mussoorie, 1991

Rejoice and come away with me
From affairs of sexuality
Come with me
Wherever I may be
Come to the valley
Of soft breezes
Whispering through misty pines
Caressing rosy hills at sunset
Dawn and twilight times.

Come to the sweet hills of Mussoorie
To roam footloose
And fancy free
Sharing in naked glory
Giving and receiving endlessly.

Himalaya on the Wall

East and West
The children roam
Till they come
To the Himalaya Mountains
Of many meditations.

The hills of Mussoorie
Return to them
In a painting
On the wall
Of their home
A long walk
from the big river:
VA 22101
Silent secret cocooned
In another country.

Home Over the Rainbow

Lovingly built of extra-large brick
Of warm shades of terracotta, sienna,
Umber, burgundy-brown.
The garnet red of the Japanese maple
To the left of the porch.
The soft veined Italian marble foyer
Of varying hues of sunburst yellows
Creamy white, vanilla, peachy-rose
Kissed by sunset shades of molten gold.
Dogwoods pink and white in the garden
And cherry blossoms in full bloom.
I turned to bid a final adieu
And walked away
Along the sloping driveway
With double azaleas of many colours
To my right and to my left
My once twenty-inch baby leyland cypresses
Grown to well over twenty feet high
To touch the clear azure sky.

I won't regret this when I die:
There was a home I loved
And when it was no longer mine
I proudly chose to say
A gracious goodbye.

Little Hut

In Osheen's little hut
In Goa
The living force
Within me
Is in harmony
With the rhythm
Of the ocean
Ebbing and flowing
Night and day
At peace with the universe.

Jasmines in the Streets

No I may not wear
Your jasmine bracelet
Upon my wrist
Such as a lover bestows
Upon his beloved.
No you may not tie
A jasmine wreath in my hair
As a husband gifts his wife.

I am more than your beloved
More than wife
You and I are all things
In and unto one another
Whole and complete
As a ring
A circle without beginning
Without end.

Before the wreath-selling children
On the street turn to go
And the traffic light turns green
I roll down the car window and buy
A dozen creamy-white jasmine wreaths
Three for ten rupees.
Perhaps then the flower-selling

Children will earn enough
To eat a meal tonight.

I sleep with a smile on my lips
Soothed by erotic fragrance
Narcotic romance
With jasmine wreaths in my hair
On my wrists ankles and feet
Among a million crushed jasmines
Strewn in the streets.

Sonnet

Underneath the spreading banyan tree
Sammy Pacher said to me
When I'm married I shall see
My husband shares a little house with me
But he'll be upstairs; I'll be down
He in the country me in the town
And once a year when we meet for tea
Oh, what a happy girl I'll be!
Underneath the spreading banyan tree
Sammy reared their family,
Some were short and very small
Others over six feet tall
This occurred so it would seem
Because they stayed at two extremes.

Sextette

Dark hair
Sparkling eyes
Endearing sighs
Fair
Fairest
In the East.

Quatrain

Lonely
Not alone
Not lonely
Alone.

Ring of Fire

A burning planet hurtling
Towards a naked sun
Spinning ever faster
Carrying people chasing
Their tails behind them
Running after
Things and tonnes of fun

Turning round and round
On a merry-go-round on fire
Having the time of their lives

On a joy ride
Within a ring of flames.

On fire.

Silk and Spice

As a ship laden with silk spice and gold
Plundered deprived and cajoled
Yields its spoils
Sighing for harbour lights
I lie wan and worn
Torn by wind and storm
Listening to ocean waves
Breaking expectantly upon
Smoothened stones on the shore
Below my balcony window.

Remembering love and hot kisses
Upon hard Deccan rocks
Black from ancient shocks
Of formation
And holding each other
Tight as ever.

Reminded of you chasing me
And our laughter
Through green paddy fields
Waving wildly in the wind
Beneath monsoon skies
Streaks of lightning

And claps of thunder
My tresses wet
In driving rain
My bosom fresh
Beneath a cambric dress.

Remembering you sailing away
On the tides of time
Over cerulean seas
Returning to me softly
In caressing waves
Quickening rushing hurtling breaking
To the rhythm of my breath
And the beating of my heart
In my sleep.

Flying

Like a bird
Hitting live electric wires
Falling rising wavering
The commuter plane
Dropped again and again
Into air pockets in the sky
And soaring
Continued to fly.

As on we flew
I knew
It would be late
To make it
To our departure gate.
I quickly said a prayer
As the plane
Plummeted again
Into a deep pocket in mid air.

White-fire lightning rent
The blackened sky
Rain fell in torrents and roared
At my porthole window
Babies began to cry

GIs swore
Wondering why
They'd ever chosen to fly
To Frankfurt through NY.

They thought they'd surely die
In the mechanical bird
Floundering low and up high.
We all felt the same way
About surviving that day
When we heard
The stewardess calmly say
We'd be okay
For our connection at JFK.

The landing of our shuttle flight
Was scheduled for half past five
What with all the delay
And afraid of losing my way
I dashed through the ramp
In pelting rain to terminal 4.
Turning to my right
I saw you standing
Waiting for me with a smile
Coming to me quickly
And holding me tight.

You melted away
My damp dismay
And fright
Making me warm cozy
And perfectly all right.

With you on the next flight
Was pure delight
Fastening my belt
And settling in my seat
On Pan Am 66
I felt excited as a child.

When our Boeing 747
Took off into the air
I didn't have a care
As long as you were there
We could be flying anywhere
With you beside me I'd roam
The world and feel at home
All the time and everywhere.

Playing

Seven thirty
On a December evening
It's raining
And maybe freezing
Tonight.

Striking the sulfur match
To pine needles and cones
Feeding logs of white ash
And maple to the fire
I watched the glowing flames
Rise and dance to clinking ice cubes
Turning golden brown with fizzing
Beaded soda bubbles
In your crystal glass.

My mind began wandering
To a distant land with you
To a time once in the blazing sun

And many a mountain
Rising fiercely
From valleys deep
To azure skies
Where we

As giants
Virtually hung on to steep
Ribbon paths
Zigzagging along claw-like cliffs
And jagged rocks
Reminding us of tigers' paws.

An untamed wilderness
All ours
Its love-hot sounds
Humming in the hush
Of sunset from dusk
To twilight hours
Till break of dawn
The vibration of its desolation
Always with us
And in the words and music
Of our songs.

Smells of ferns and leaves
Of various greens
Umbers purples greys
And ultramarines
Of flowers stones rocks
Shrubs and trees
And ever-changing shades

Of rivers skies brooks streams
And endless tops
Of silent hills
Vibrant in the darkness
Enfolding us calm and still.

Both of us watching
Our souls leave our bodies
Pour out like liquid silver
Into the moonlight
And dancing in union with creation
Over forests huts and rills along
Rippling brooks and creeks
Flowing full and strong
Night and day long.

Our waking and sleeping
Becoming one
Our eating drinking resting
And moving on
Resonating
To an everlasting harmony
Of being-ness
In a unified existence
Hardly ever known.

And there I saw your glory
And you saw mine
Lush as a verdant valley
Giving and receiving naturally
You and I isolated among
Hot boulders and glittering sand
Beneath a burnished sun
In a burning sky
With ice-cold waters
Running swiftly by.

Mixed smells of wood and weed
Towering peaks on all sides
And forests where cobras
And tigers hide
Without a soul in sight for miles
With you singing
In the wilderness by my side.
Strumming your guitar
In your printed boxer underwear
Your body bare
Watching over me asleep
Without a care
Wearing your khaki shorts
And my skimpy white chemise.

Waking slowly with the sun in my eyes
And you standing astride above me
Asking with the sweetest of smiles
If I needed a drink
And contriving to drip
Sweet mango juice bit by bit
Through a straw onto my lips.

Both of us bursting out laughing
In fits at this
Our way of creating
Our own reality
Of you playing with my sensuality
And I playing
With your personality.

Spout Run

Putting down my book
Of the poems of John Donne
I gaze across the blue heavens
To a faint runway of National Airport.
Watching planes take off to my left
Over swiftly flowing shiny waters
Of the River Potomac
Churning to my right.

Looking below
From the glass-front window
Of the lounge
On the fifth floor
Of Lauinger Library
And breaking free
Of papers for a degree
I leap out and reach across
To touch the tip
Of the massive arch
Spanning Spout Run opposite me.

I climb over dark rocks
And boulders
Overhanging lush vines
And dense trees
Beyond and beneath
Which I cannot see.

I gaze inwardly
At our enchanted laughter
And our dancing briefly
At a parting of ways
Believing all roads to be
Converging ultimately at the centre
Of a universe in our beings.

We go travelling
Under bridges over ditches
Of our destinies
Crossing crossings
Without intersecting
As the living dead
Within narrow confines
Of time present past and future
All gone and done
With John Donne.

Your Face

Your face is the face
I chase through sunny clouds
In flowery meadows
Of childhood days.

Your shape is the shape
That takes
My arm in his
And walks with me to plays
Dance halls and cafes
Of girlhood days.

Your form is the form
That stays
With me in the storm
Of womanhood days.

Your face is the face
Form and shape
I chase
In starry skies
On moonlit ocean waves.

You are a vapour
Vanishing in the rain
I trace reflections
Of your beloved face
Among rainbows
In blue heavens
And silver clouds sailing by
On golden days.

Washingtonian Chant*

In the name
Of my Mother
The Father
And of the Son
I pray *Ek Omkaar*
Sat Naam.

I map the flames of Nine Eleven
Om
They seem the same
Bhur
As those of Nineteen Forty-Seven
Bhuva
I'm crisscrossed with Equality
Svaaha
Liberty and Justice for all

---

*The poem incorporates the Gayatri Mantra of Brahma Rishi Vishvamitra:
Om bhur bhuva svaaha
Tat savi tur varenyam
Bhargo de vasya dhi mahi
Deeyo yo na prachodayaat.
You, the Creator, give us birth, protect and nurture us with life.
From you we receive our breath.
You end sufferers' woes.
Your greatness shines supreme and out of which the earth exists.
You are present in all Creation and everything.
I meditate upon you.
I ask for your grace in guiding my understanding
To walk upon the path of the highest goodness.)

Tat
I'm marked by the Fourth of July
Savi
August Fifteenth
Tur
Halloween
Varenyam
Diwali
Bhargo.

All turn out the same.

The CIA
De
Diagonally across my backyard
Vasya
The Golden Temple
Dhi
The Capital
Mahi
The Taj Mahal
Dheeyo
The White House
Yo
Dance deflected in my sleep
Na

Among pink cherry blossoms
Pracho
Reflected on the Pond
Dayaat
At Washington Mall.

I cut the festered knot
And chant mantras
Ending up in the same
Holy name.

Among Marble Mansions the Flowers Died

It was afternoon in the colony of marble mansions when
The fire broke out inside the 'Ferns and Petals' flower shop
From careless electrical connections commonly done.
The innocent fresh flowers died quickly in the flames.
The ancient neem tree's lofty branches
Reached out like generous arms across the street
Taking the smoke unto themselves—
Unsinged. As did the thick leaves
Of the chubby rubber tree.
And the stout simal with red flowers
The soaring bougainvillea
And madhu malti vines
All stood like sentinels along
The railing wall and took it upon
Themselves to inhale the smokey fumes
And protect the air and keep it clean
Within the two humble green acres of E Pachaas
No. W4/19—the date I was born a tree.

Clearly the Forest

I close my eyes and see clearly
The shimmering forest alive
Beneath the two acres
As it was before it got trodden upon
Buried and choked by the concrete
Of human greed.
I know where the cows
Came to drink water
In the natural *haud*
By the boundary railing.
I hear their cowbells
From a hundred years ago.

Khabar

Hawa ke jhonke mein
Guzarti soch le kar
Dil dhoondta hai vo ghar
Baagh Sardaaraan
Dingee Khooee ke *kareeb*
Main road paar
Chauree see gali mein
Saamne dukaanein.
Aage kuchh kadam par gurdwara
Jo kabh khatm kar diya jaaye
Kaun jaane, aur kaun jaane
Vo khoobsurat ghar
Kis haalat mein ho aur kab
Apni hee mitti mein dhal jaye
Rawalpindi se khabar aaye na aaye.

(The passing breeze carries a vagrant thought
And my heart looks for a house: Bagh Sardaran
Near the Dingee Well, across the main road
In the broad gali facing the shops.
Just a few paces ahead, a gurdwara
Which might be razed to the ground some day

Who knows when, and who knows
The fate of that beautiful home and how long
Before it returns to the dust that it was
While we wait for news from Rawalpindi.)

Distant Shores

Trusting and believing
Let's go through eternity
Keeping close to each other
We are strangers
In a strange country.

Spread out flat beside each other
On hot red stone slabs
Of the Fort of Agra
Walking barefoot in the moonlight
On the smooth cool white marble
Of the Taj Mahal.

Sprawled on a colossal bed
Of the Lake Palace
Sharing stories
Unravelling life's mysteries
Watching worlds gone by
Through myriad floral arches.

Trusting and believing
Let's go through eternity
Keeping close to each other
We are strangers
In a strange country.

Eternal Light

'When I stand upright in the wind,
My bones turn to dark emeralds.'

—David Wright, 'The Jewel'

I stepped out of the charcoal black
Metallic Jaguar with the wind in my face
The sun falling on my back
The moon and stars upon my shoulder
My spine became upright
Turned into a pillar of emeralds.
No one is going to touch the blossom
Of fire within my womb
The Paramjyot, the Supreme Light
Of Creation.

Picture Credits

Painting on page 3—'Round Sunflower'—by Anselmus de Boodt; painting on page 25 by Nicholas Roerich; paintings on pages 7 and 26 by the author; painting on page 29—'The Horse and the Lioness'—by George Stubbs.

Photo on page 13—'Rain Song'—by Anjali Budakoti; on page 14—'Sunset in Jastarnia Beach'—by Diego Delso; on page 18—'Sunset Lakshman Jhoola, Rishikesh'—by Tylersundance; on page 30—'Yamuna River at Yamunotri'—by Atarax; on page 46, of Arambol Beach, Goa by Riddinghag; on page 52—'Beach and the Lonely Lighthouse'—by Somaliyaswan; on page 79—'Shiva as the Lord of Dance', from the LACMA collection. All sourced from Wikimedia Commons.